COLORING
ANIMAL MANDALAS

Wendy Piersall

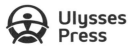
Ulysses
Press

Published by
Ulysses Press
P.O. Box 3440
Berkeley, CA 94703
www.ulyssespress.com

ISBN: 978-1-61243-350-9

Printed in Canada by Marquis Book Printing

10 9 8 7 6 5 4 3

Acquisitions editor: Kelly Reed
Managing editor: Claire Chun
Front cover design: what!design@whatweb.com

Distributed by Publishers Group West

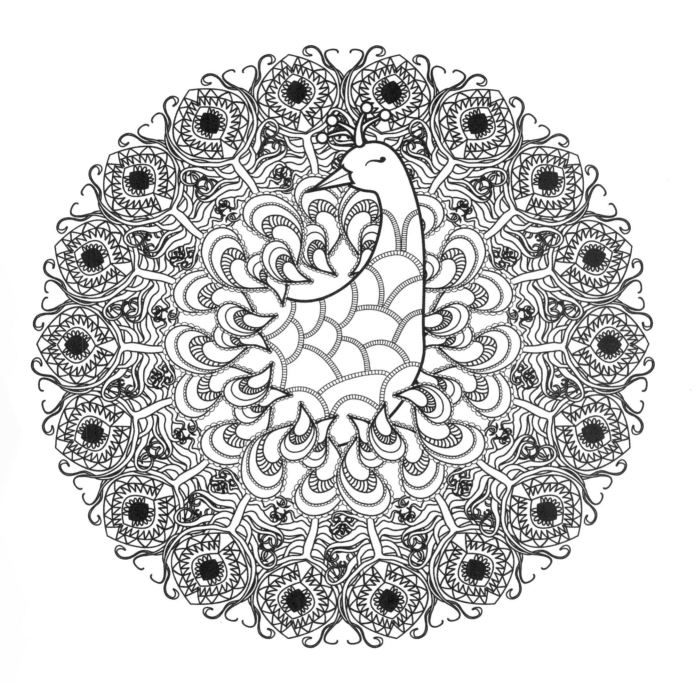

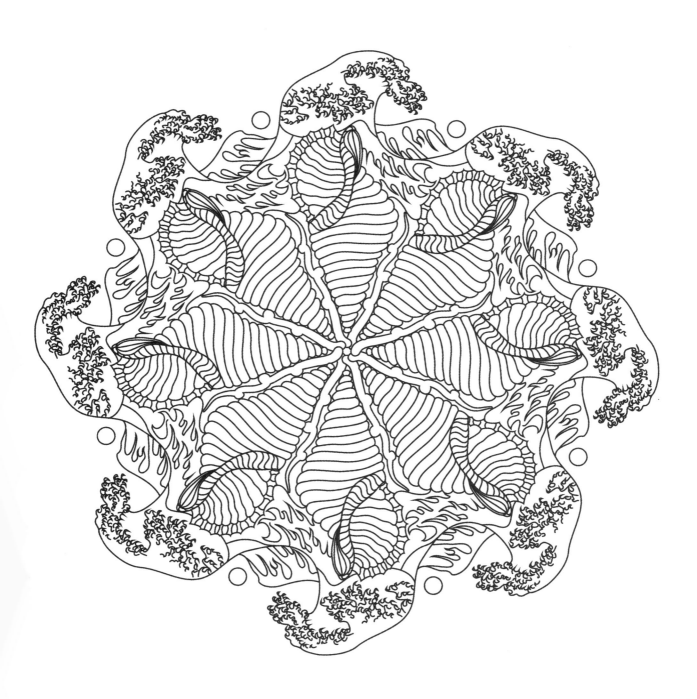

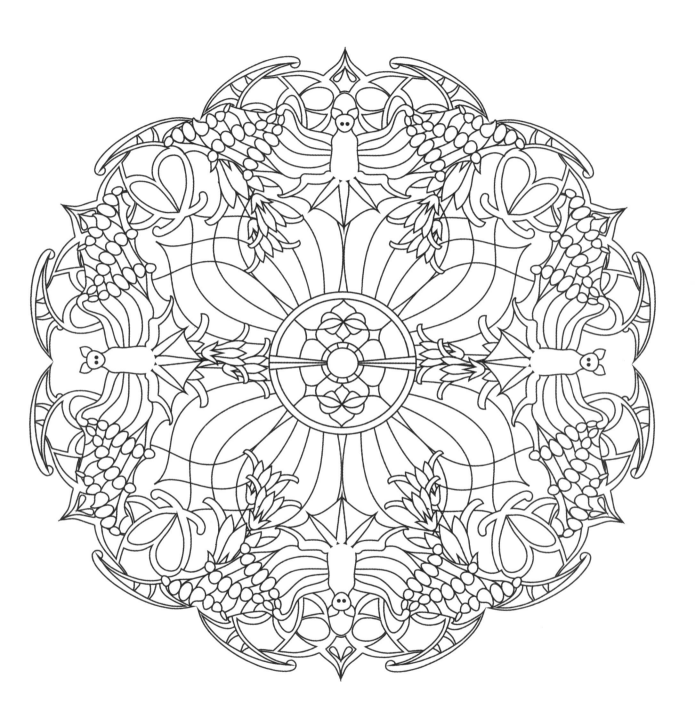

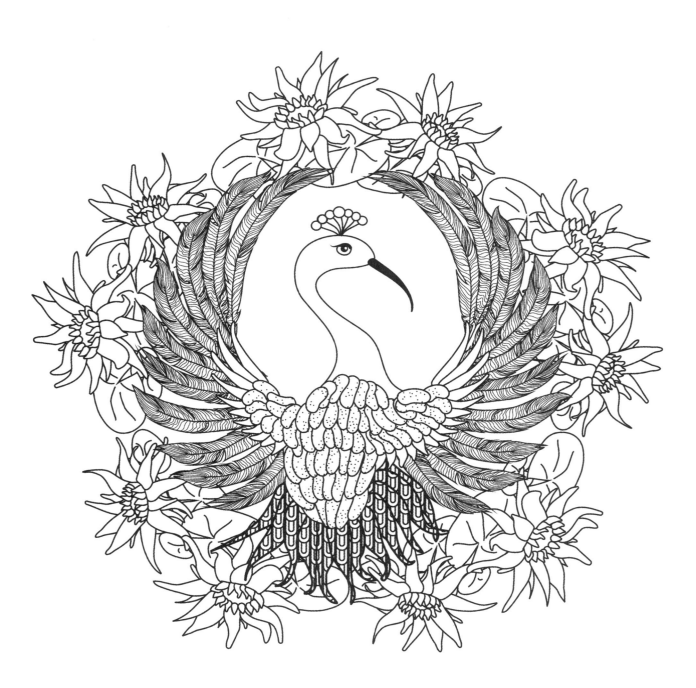

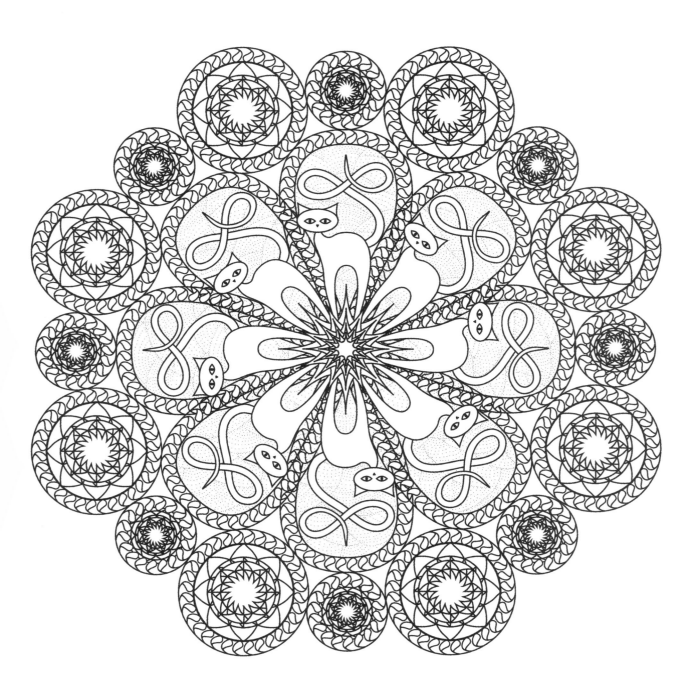

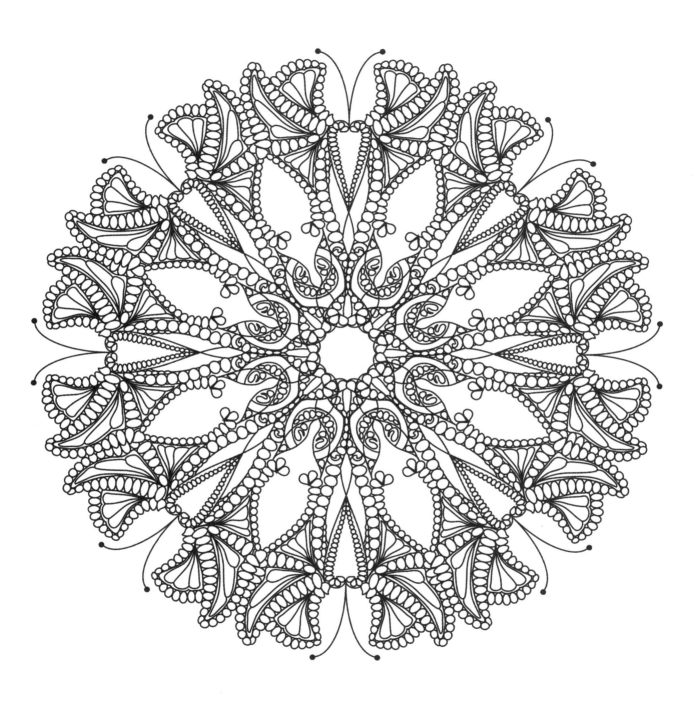

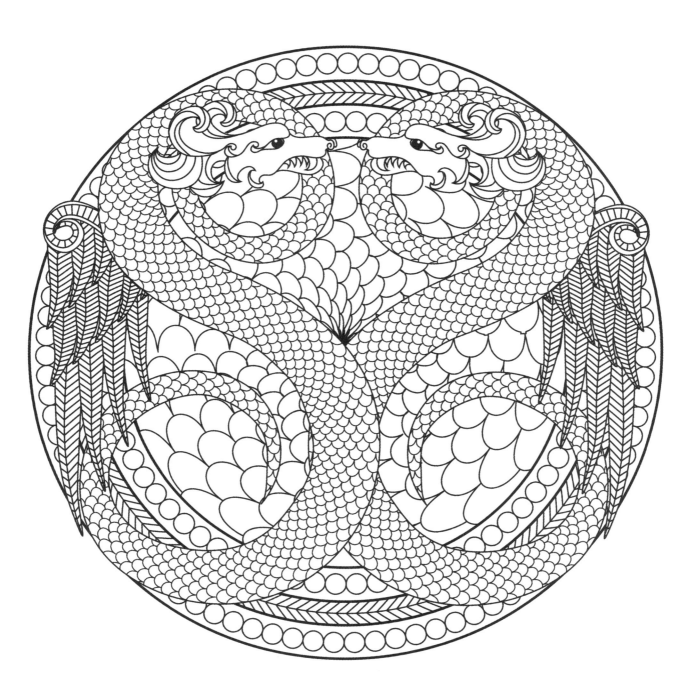

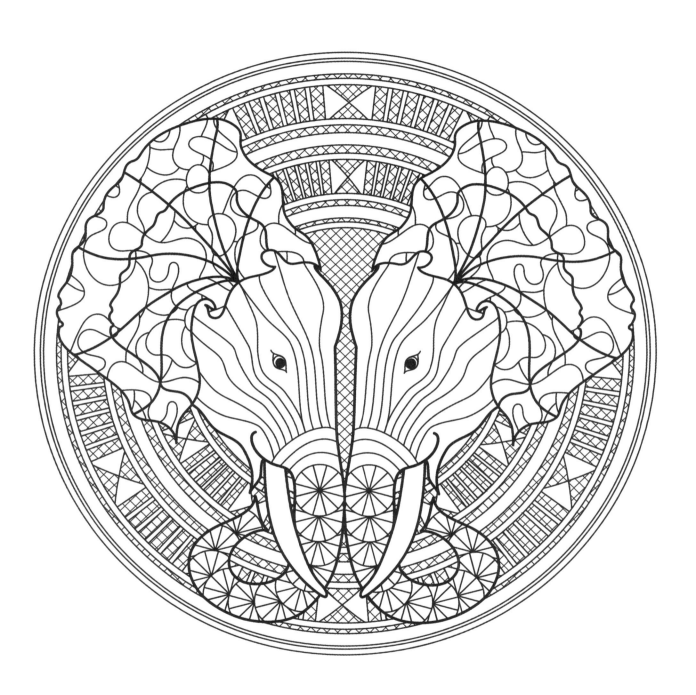

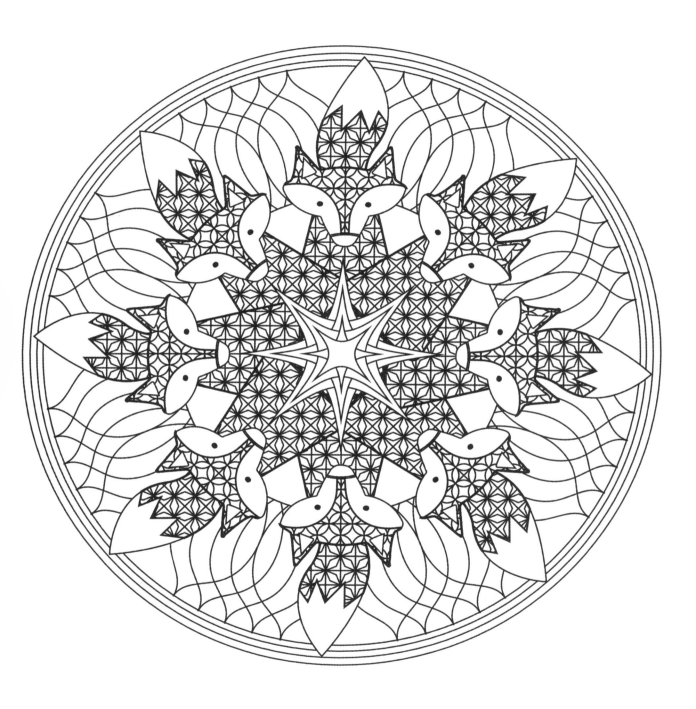

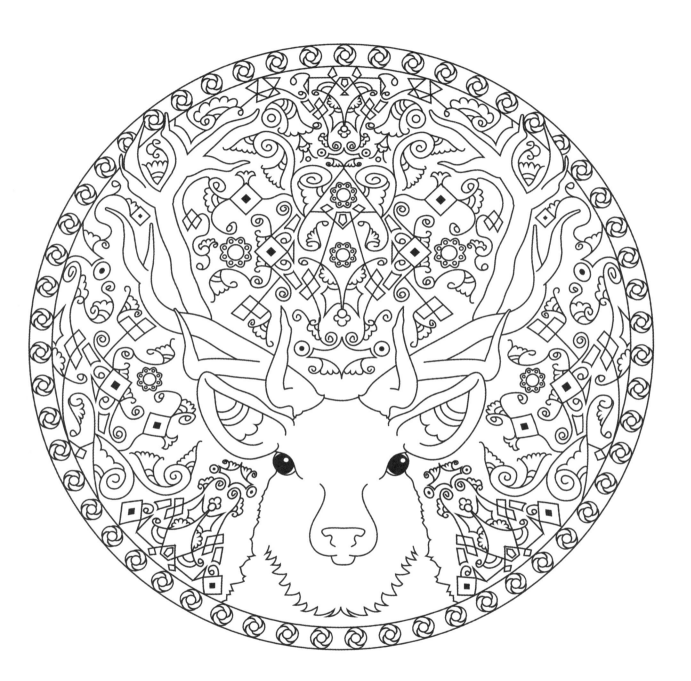

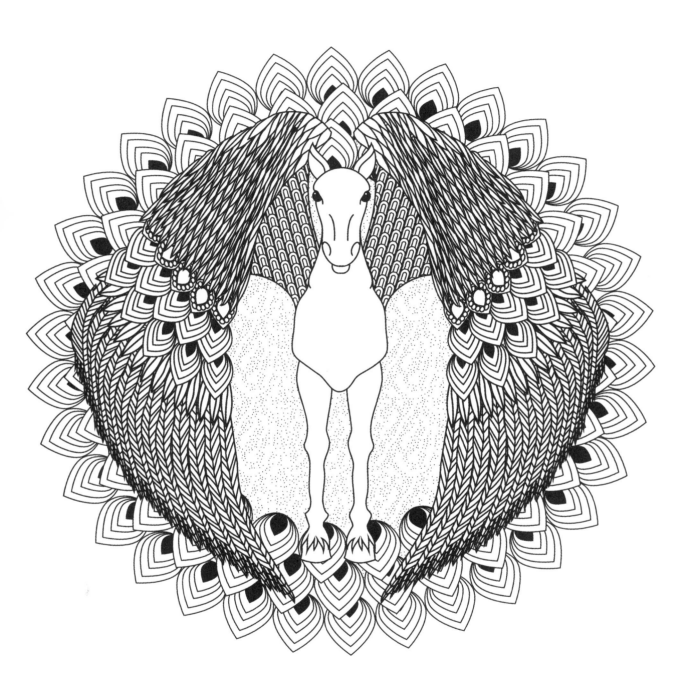

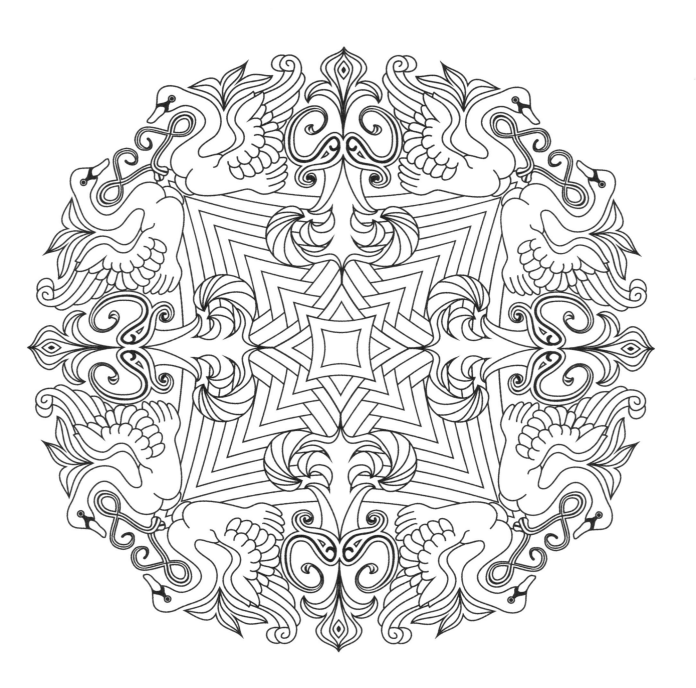

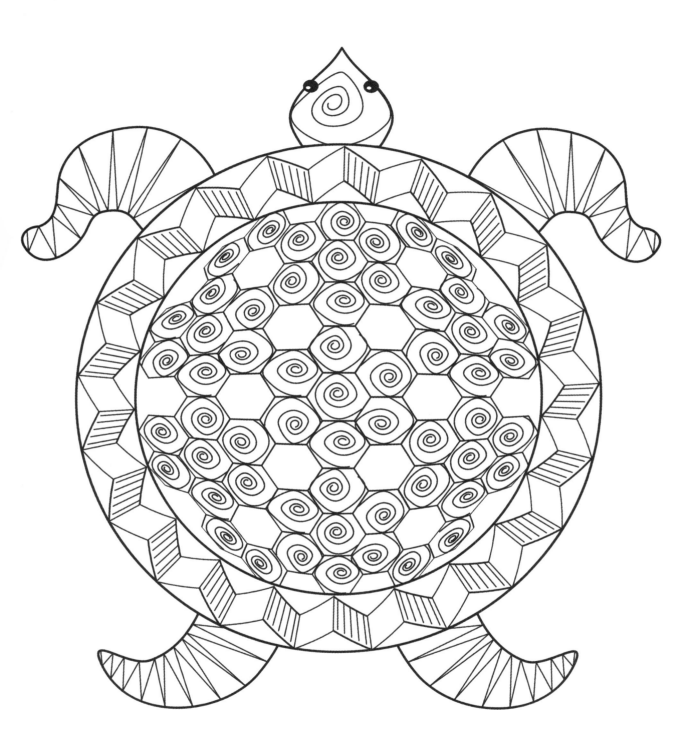

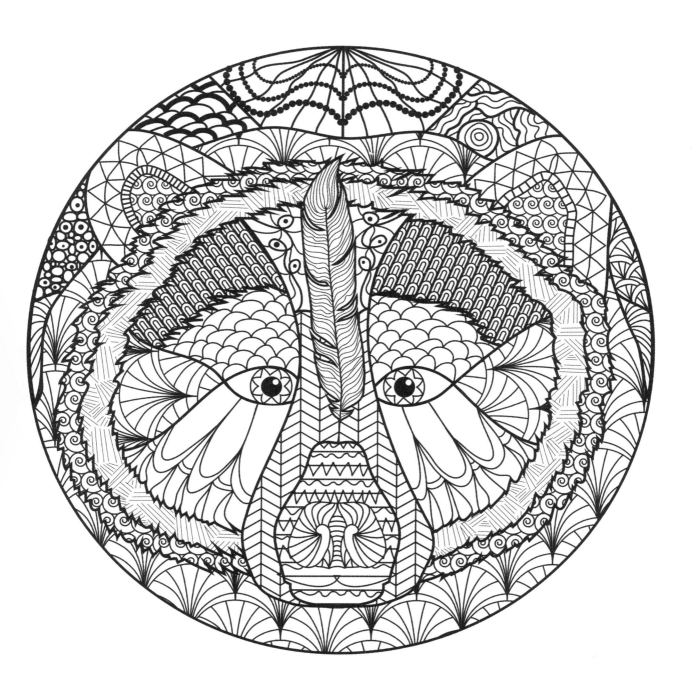

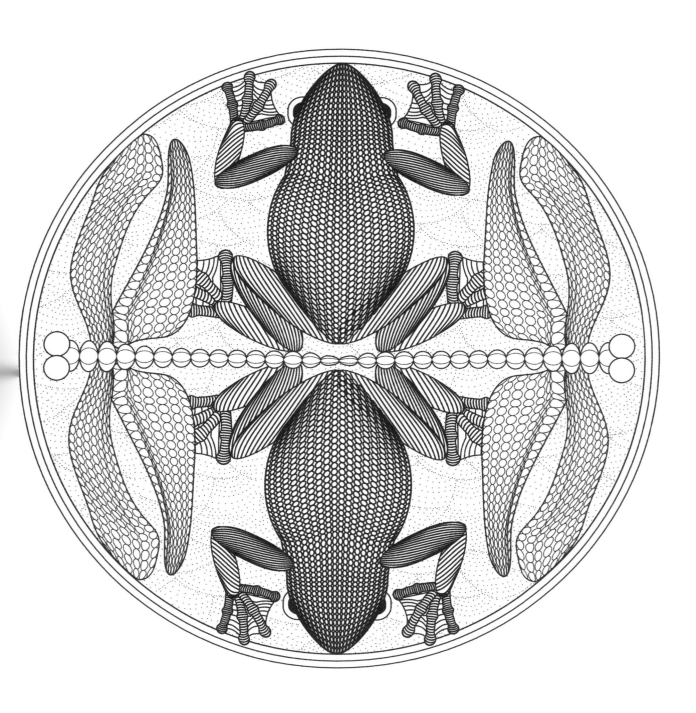

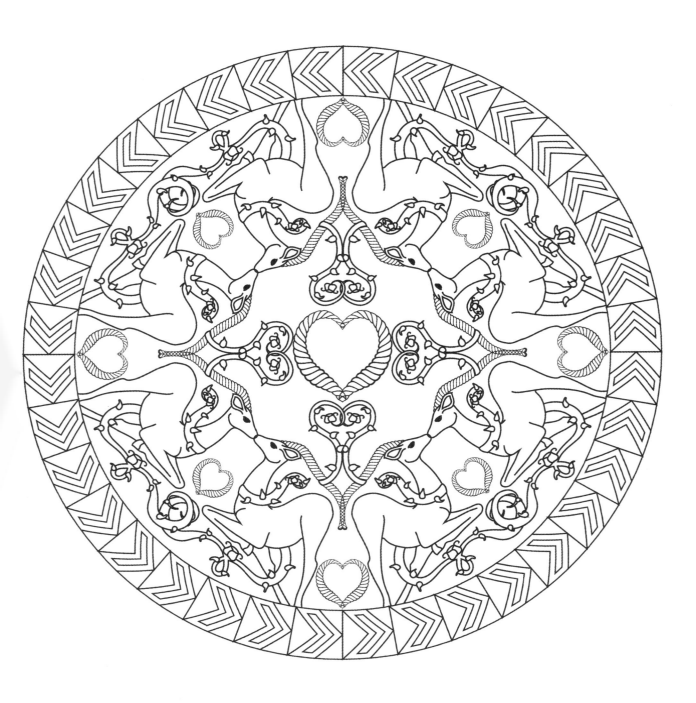

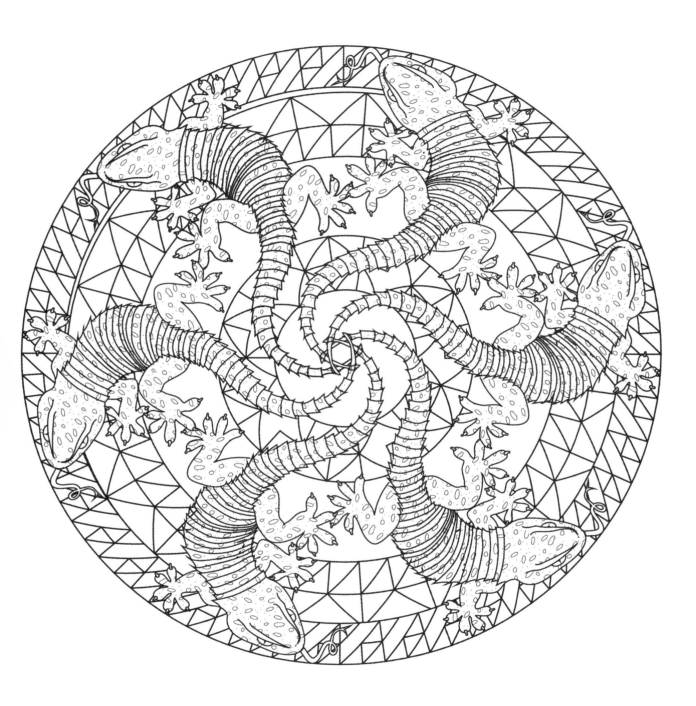

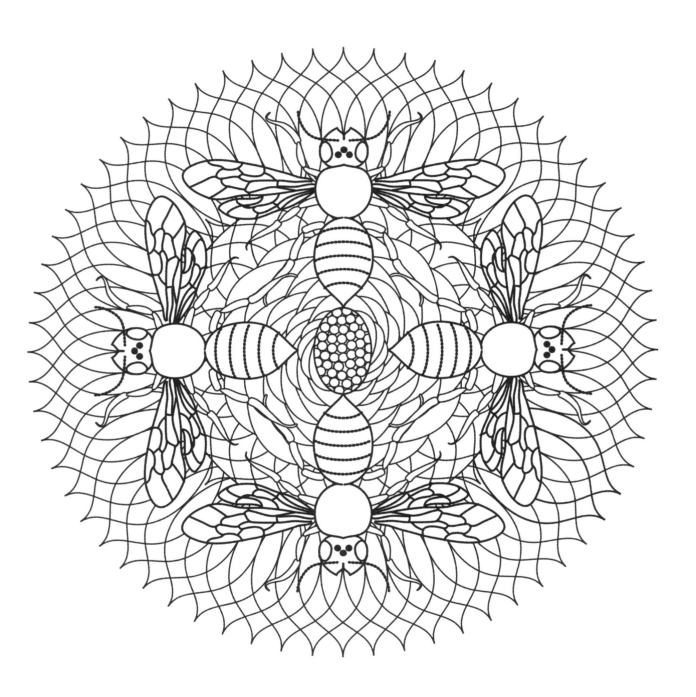

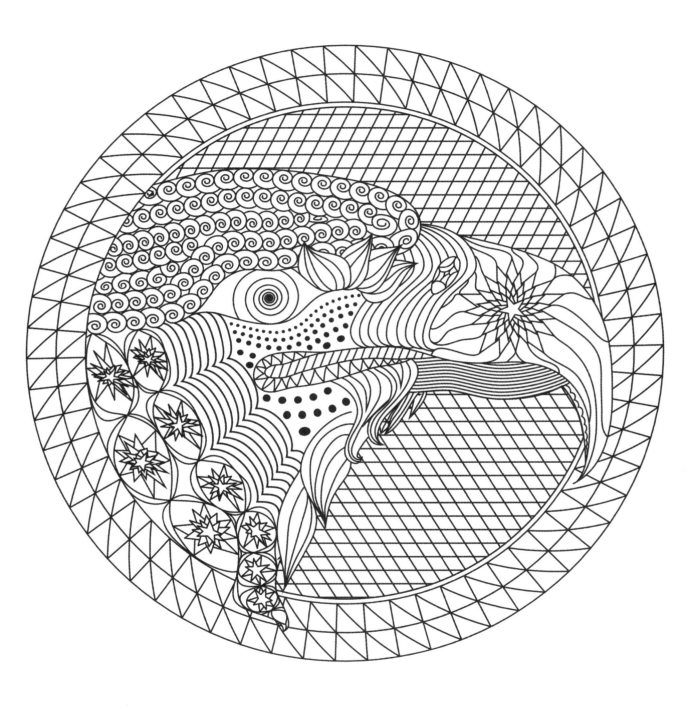

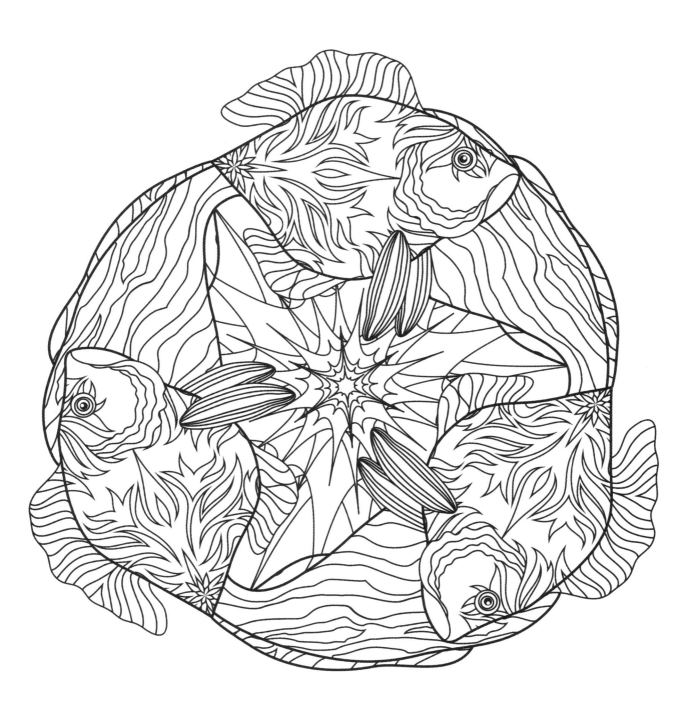

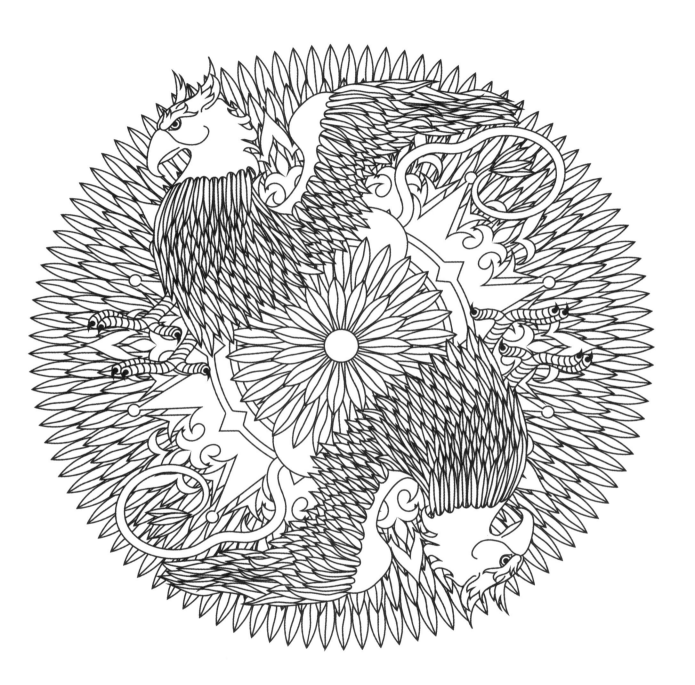

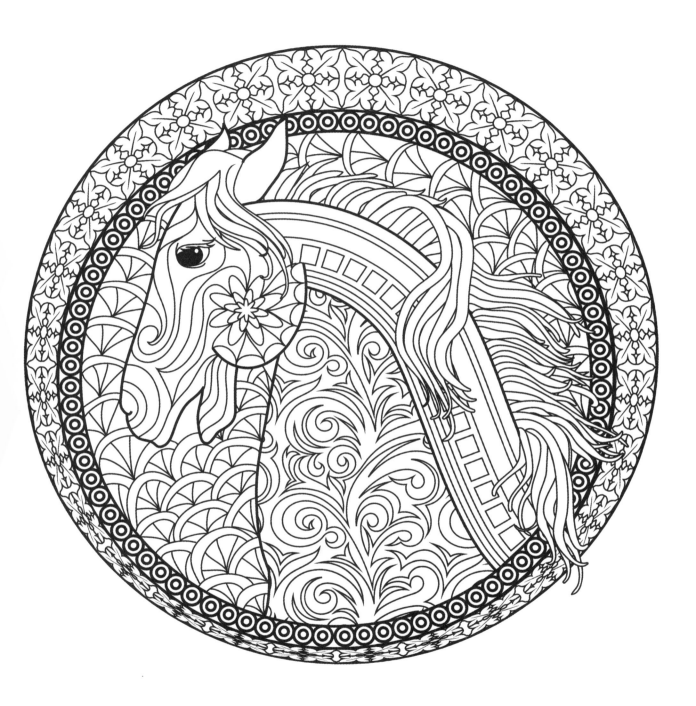

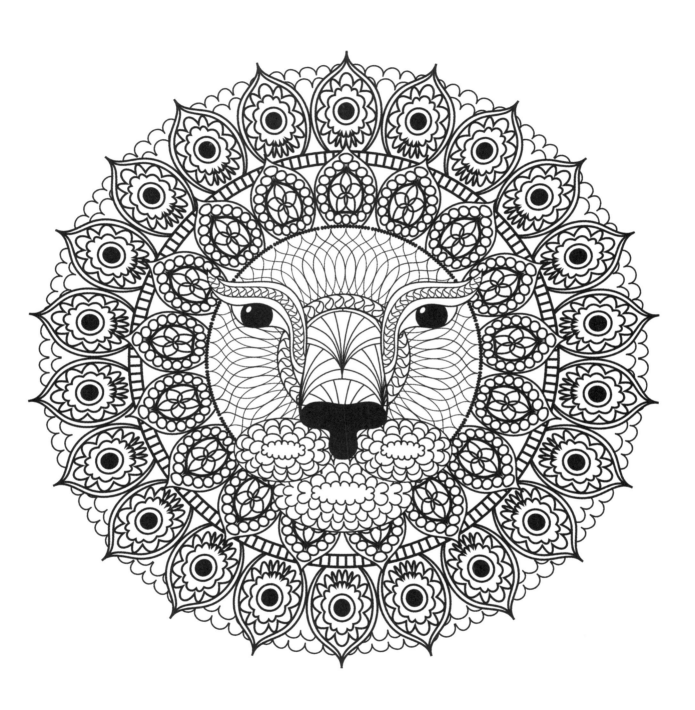

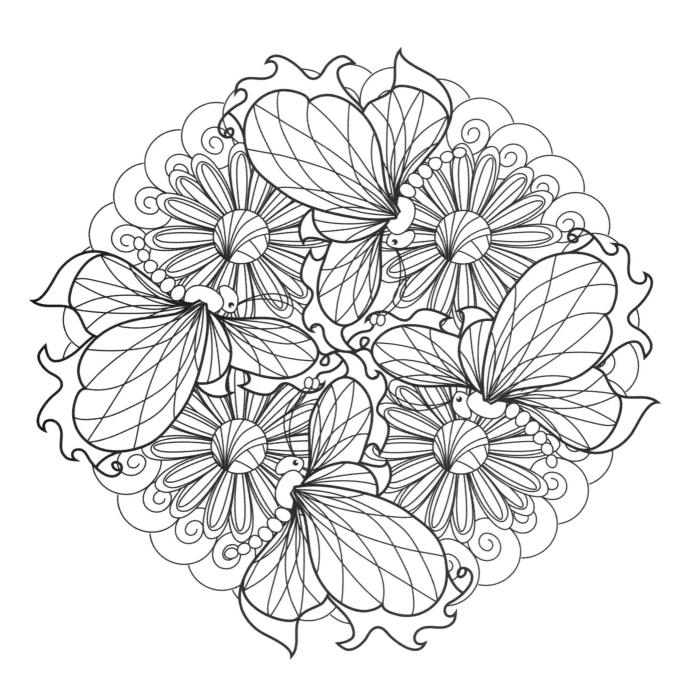

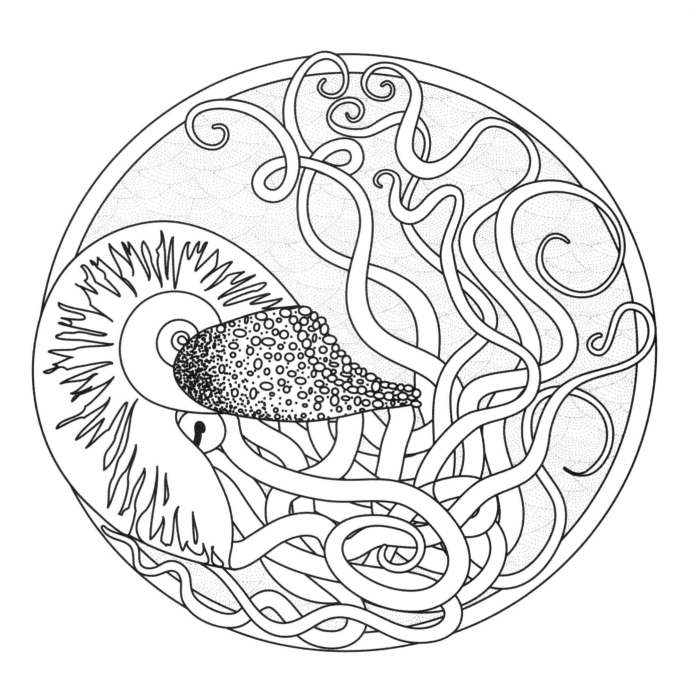

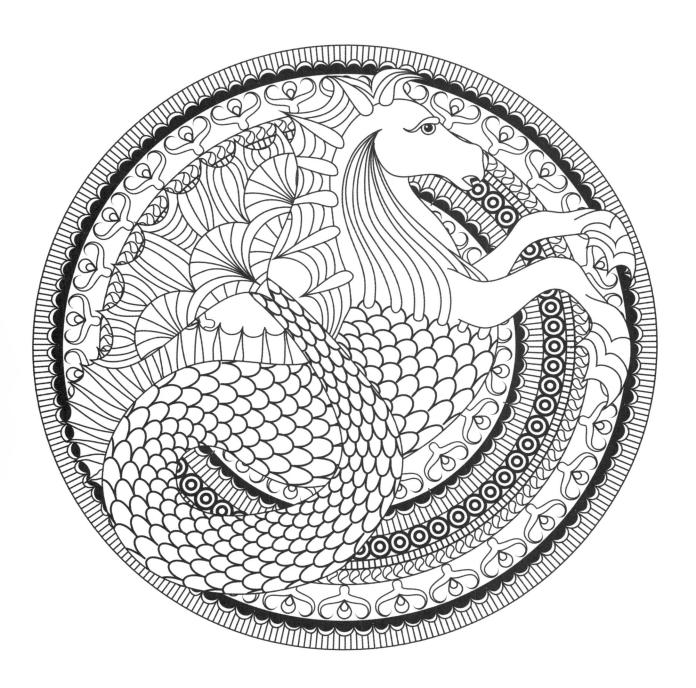

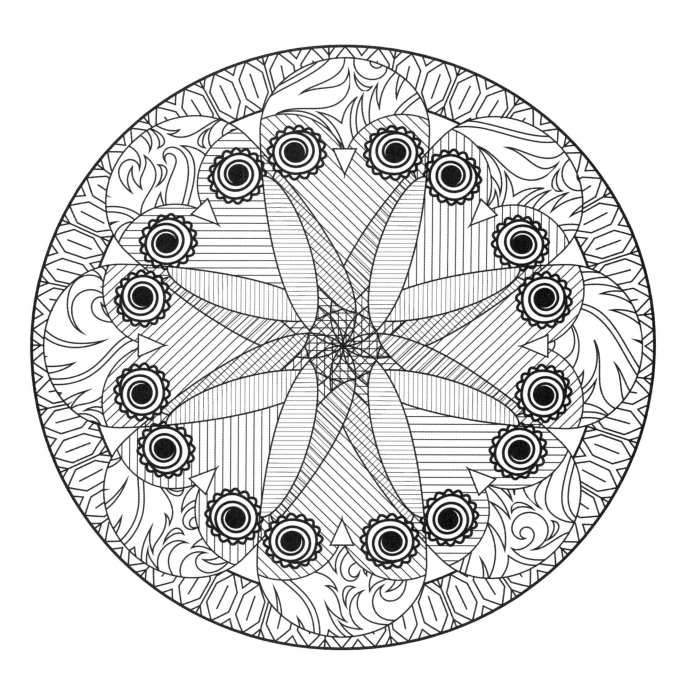

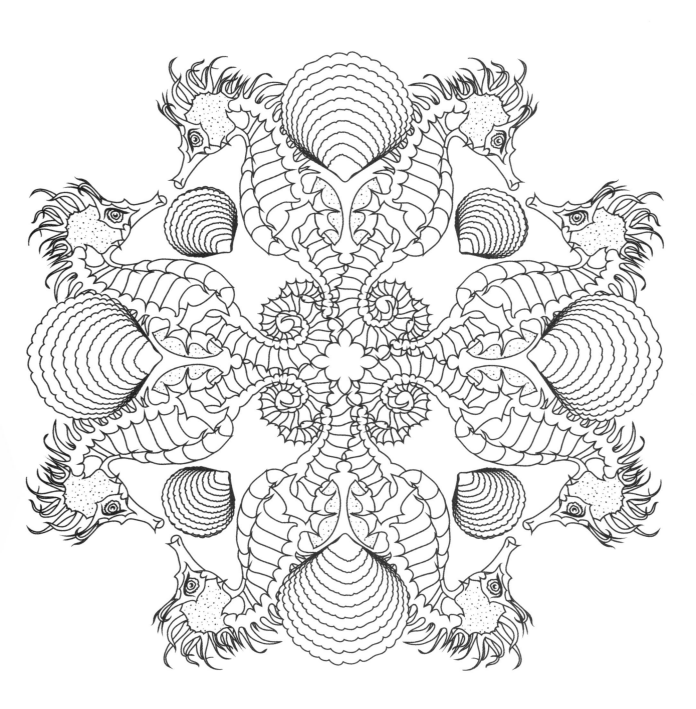

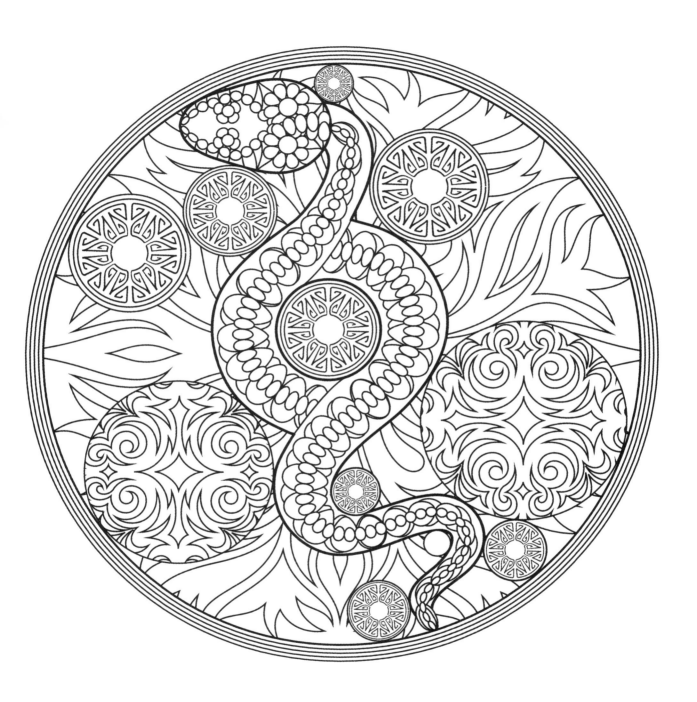

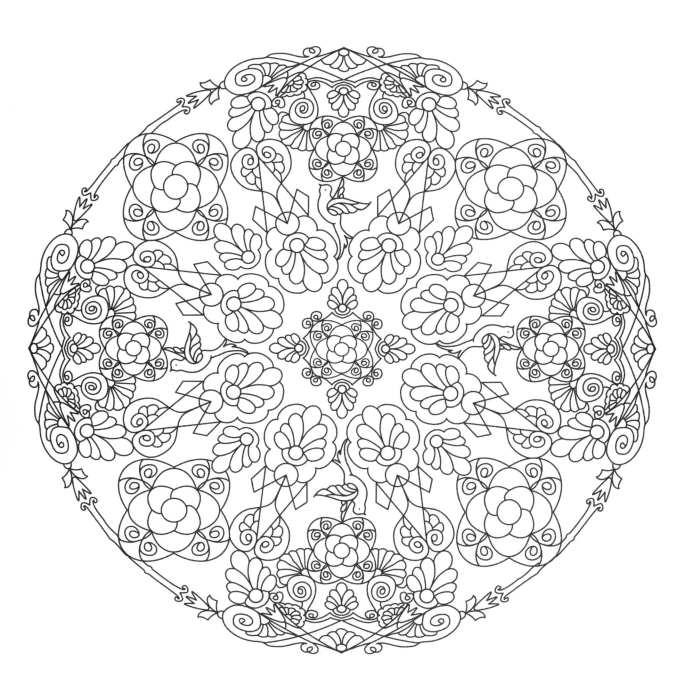

ABOUT THE ILLUSTRATOR

Wendy Piersall is a lifelong artist with over 17 years of professional design experience. She has been drawing mandala coloring pages as the founder of the Woo! Jr. Kids Activities website for kids since 2009. She lives with her husband and three children in Woodstock, Illinois.